GOD'S
COUNTRY

GOD'S COUNTRY

Poems by
Joseph J Smith

Writhm.com

Writhm
Writhm.com

Printed in the United States of America
10 9 8 7 6 5 4 3 2 1

Dedicated to the beautiful memory of my loving mother, Naomi Smith, and to my neices and nephews who are like my children and especially my neice, Abria Smith, who helped to make this book possible.

Contents

I Will Be Free.. 10

Little Brown Cow 11

Oh Mother Nature 12

Darling You Know It's True 13

The Tulips 14

The Saddle Up 15

Blossom 16

Your True Loving... 17

Twinkle Twinkle.. 18

God's Work.. 19

Thanksgiving Day... 21

A New Bike for Friddie on Easter......................... 22

Valentine... 23

Childish Love 24

Tender Love.. 25

The Moon at Night 26

Valentine's Day 27

When Love is Divided.................................... 28

While the Moon is Bright 29

Mother's Day... 30

Father's Day.. 31

The Stars 32

Birds Outside the Window................................ 33

A Little Christmas Tree................................... 34

Peace of God 35

My Childhood Days....................................... 37

Peace Be with You....................................... 38

God Be With You 39

My Love 42

Gifts Under the Tree..................................... 43

Jupiter... 44

The Shadow of Love 45
John F. Kennedy. 46
Happy Easter 47
Thankful for Easter 48
Little Stream. 49
The Stair Steps of Heaven. 50
Joe Louis. 51
Love is Like a Rainbow 52
Little Brown Cow 2. 53
I Am the Man in Your Dreams 54
Rose. 55
The Gift of Wisdom 56
The Little Tree. 57
Stars 58
My Home Town. 59
Angels Sang 60
Fourth of July Fun 61
Mothers Day 62
Joy. 63
The Touch of Your Hand 64
To Grow Old. 65
My True Love. 66
You. 67
The Little Harp 68
I Lost a Love. 69
Roses in the Garden 70
Listen to God's Voice 71
God, Maker of Pure Life 72
Falling Tears 73
Let's Call Love 74
My Heart Hurts So Bad. 75
Queen to Wed 76
America 77

Sun 78

The Cat 79

Trust in God 80

Jackie 81

The Candle. 82

God Made You For Me 83

Sharing 84

The Little Old Train. 85

Fruitful Little Tree 86

Friendship. 87

A Tear Falls 88

Let's Fall in Love 89

A Rose to My Mother 90

Always Young 91

Christmas. 92

Beautiful Christmas Tree 93

Christmas Heaven 94

Joy Bells 95

Love Travels. 96

Super Fine 97

All My Love for You 98

Your Love 99

All of the People Know 100

Love That Has Saddened Me. 101

Why I Was Born 102

Let's Make Love by the Fireplace 103

Diamond Rings of Gold. 104

Love is Not the Blame. 105

Joy Comes Every Day 106

Watch Your Steps 107

Growing Old 108

Lost and Found 109

I Will Be Free

When the maker comes and calls me
I will be free of all hatred and poverty
I will be like the birds and the bees
I will be free in heaven
Then I and the angels will lend a helping hand
To get rid of the devil and his man
I will be free when the maker comes
Play on the horns and play on the drums
When the angels cry blow your horn
Get rid of the wall and all of the thorns
Because I will be free to sail at last
And forget the heart and pass
I will be free to sing and play
When the angels in heaven come to rescue me
The maker will give me a helping hand
To get rid of the wickedness
And bring peace and harmony
I will be free

Little Brown Cow

Little brown cow sitting all alone
Little brown cow, where is your home
Little brown cow, you give milk all along
Little brown cow, sing me a song
Before you leave home
Little brown cow, have you a little cow
Eating in the grass
How much time has passed
Little brown cow, go a week and walk a mile
Sometimes you help the farmer plow
And eat the grass for miles and miles
Little brown cow wagging his tail
And giving the children a big smile
Little brown cow is it worthwhile
Send the brother a cow
Give him a hand
They send his milk to Paris in France
Let's give him a great big hand
We had bacon and ham in the pan
Raise no sand, let's give him another hand
Wash the dishes and the pans
Lots of milk goes to France
Little brown cow
Bark bark and meow
Little brown cow I hate to say goodbye
But time sure does fly
Little brown cow, goodbye, goodbye.

Oh Mother Nature

Mother nature why are you late
Mother nature but you are so great
Mother nature set the world in bloom
Mother nature I saw you zoom
Mother nature gave me a home
Now I do not have to roam
I have found a house that is made of foam
Like great music that came from home
I ate chicken down to the bone
I like music and all kinds of love songs
Mother nature come on strong
I don't really know how I go on
The stars are always glowing
My sister is always sewing
Outside, it's always snowing
Where is little Joey
He's such such a good boy
Mother nature come to my side
Many times I've cried
Mother nature be my friend
Mother nature ride on the wind

Darling You Know It's True

Darling you know it's true
Sweet baby I love only you
So don't make me sad or blue
Baby I am so in love with you
So please tell me we are not through.
Darling you know it's true, that I love only you
So please don't do me wrong,
Let me sing you a sweet song
Darling it's true because I really love you.
Darling it's true, all of the love I give to you.
So please don't make me sad or blue
Because you know that I love only you.
Darling it's true that I really love only you.
So please don't do me wrong
And let me sing this happy song,
So that we can carry on.
Darling you know it's true, that I really want you
Tell me my love is never through.
So don't make me blue because
I am so in love with you.
So give me a kiss or two
Baby say that we are never through
And I want to make love to you
Why are you so untrue
Give me a kiss, one two. Cause
You know that I love only you.
Let me make love to only you.
Because I am so in love with you.

The Tulips

The tulips that I bought
They are such a beautiful thought.
When you play you get caught.
The tulip
Has such a beautiful
smile and glow.
That's why I bought a row.
They don't grow in the cold.
I love to see them in rows
when they have a tulip in every end
and every bend.

The Saddle Up

A saddle hanging in the barn
looks like it hasn't been worn,
It is beautiful golden and brown,
I hope it's for me.
I will love it forever more.
I will cherish it with great pride.
I will saddle up on my horse
And ride with great pride
Giddy up pony, let's ride
Into the sunset we must ride
Giddy up horse
We must ride through the valleys
And countryside
With my new saddle
I must ride
Through the countryside
Like a cowboy riding high
With my hat on the side
My fancy boots shining in the sun,
I will click my heel on the side,
Let's go pony and ride.
Giddy up pony
It's time to roam the whole countryside
Over hills and valleys
Into the sunset with pride.

Blossom

Blossom on a tree,
Beautiful as can be.
All of the blossoms were made for you and me.
Blossoms are made to admire and love...
To eat the beauty of its sweet taste.
There are blossoms of many colors,
Yellow, purple and green,
Even the rainbows in the sky have a picture
blooming into the most beautiful colors in the summer
and disappear until next year
It's Nature's Way of Showing
a display for the world to see.

Your True Loving

Your true loving is
Just for me girl
You make me feel like I am in a world of fancy
No one has ever made me feel like I'm
On a cloud
Stars in my eyes at night,
Lights in the heavens with a glow
There is no other way I can explain that,
You're an angel from above.
You brighten up every day. All my tears
Dried up in my eyes. This joy I can't explain
Like a miracle heaven sent
From above,
A diamond in the sky.

Twinkle Twinkle

Twinkle twinkle little star
Now I know who you are.
Lady you're my lucky star,
You were born for only me,
Your love can warm the chill of the night.
I love to feel your warm embrace
Around my shoulders
Your kisses printed on my face with lipstick
Painted ruby red.
You make my heart beat with the silk beauty
Of your touch.
You're the true love just for me.

God's Work

God's work is fine
He created earth on time like an ocean.
Heaven poured out his grace to create life.
The stars, moon and sun to show
the view of the heavens light
The sea cloud of his glory
Filled with the silky pillow
Soft and white, blue, gray
And while he crowded the heaven in the sky
Rain fell to fill the sea, oceans with blue waters,
clear as the sky. Trees plants and flower seeds
Bloomed in heavenly colors,
For the world to see,
Blades of grass carpet green,
Filled the land like
A blanket colored green.
Popcorn seeds bursting in flowers
everywhere on earth, animals hide in dens,
Keeping the newborn warm,
With hairy coats.
Hidden in the grass,
Animals of different kinds of life
Beautiful is the handiwork of God,
babies born of all creatures,
Great and small. Living creatures jumping
In the water to swim,
Birds flying overhead in the heavenly sky,
Hills high and low touch the sky above,
And the smell of heaven's garden throughout
The Earth, the aroma of God's grace

Painting his own display for us to see
He blessed all mankind to live in the garden
Where angels live.
They guard day and night without rest
Keeping watch over us.
A world of beauty he created by hand.
A part of beauty for all living things.

Thanksgiving Day

Thanksgiving Day, I hope to be there,
To join the family affairs.
We will have turkey, cranberry sauce, potato salad,
Greens, sweet potato pie.
Plenty of refreshing drinks: Apple cider,
Or drinks of wine and cola.
I know family and friends will all be there
Singing and dancing, laughter and fun.
We will give grace with prayer as we
Join, at the table to eat
Hoping to see you each year.

A New Bike for Friddie on Easter

Friddie's Easter surprise
Was a new bike painted red.
He was filled with delight.
It was so bright,
Shining like a sunny day.
In its basket was a rabbit,
Fuzzy and white, packed with candy.
Jelly beans, rainbow colors of every kind,
Easter eggs blue, white, purple, to eat all day.
I love Easter
Not only for baskets filled with candy.
I know the true meaning
Is the gift of Christ.

Valentine

Please give me a card
Saying I love you, from the heart that is true,
Take a little time and say kind words.
I will give you a card that is kind and true,
Saying I love you.
Let's take time and read to each other
With kind words from our hearts,
Words are good, sweet, like chocolate candy,
Good to eat,
Let us share our love with sweet thoughts, love.

Childish Love

Why do you make me so blue,
When I give all my love to you.
I want to hold you in my arms,,
And never let you go.
Fill you with all of my charm,
With kisses all in a row.
Your lips are like roses on a vine,
So sweet, like wine.
I will never stop loving you, you are my
First and childhood love.
You're the fresh cherry on a bush,
That was tasted with my love.
You are still my dream at night,
sent by the heavens up above.

Tender Love

Handle my tender love with care,
It's an easily broken glass.
Let me fill your heart with loving care,
And tender love.

With you in my arms,
my life is filled with joy.
And music fills the air.
You're the music of my
Beating heart, without it
My heart is silent in the night
With loneliness, and pain,
tears fall on my pillow through the night.

You visit my dream day and night,
your perfume is still on my pillow.
You promised to always be on my mind,
Yet you left me crying.
My heart is shattered like broken glass,
in a thousand pieces that
Can't be fixed until you
Come back into my life,
My heart will die of
Loneliness.

Will you come to this empty heart,
My door is open to your heart
The key to my heart has
Never changed, only you can open the door
That has been closed
Without your love.

The Moon at Night

Have you ever walked in the night
Where there wasn't even light
The moon was out of sight
And darkness dropped its shades at night.
There wasn't a speck of light
There before your eyes appeared
Like a star, that showed its heavenly light
A starburst like a diamond pearl from
A goldmine in the sky.
Shined with riches as heavenly light
One star lights the heaven with
God's pure light
Darkness will never overcome heaven's light.

Valentine's Day

Valentine's Day is for love and lovers,
To express their love. With warmth.
Feeling true love, sharing cards,
and boxes filled with candy.
Giving roses, red like wine, as gifts
to their sweethearts.

Hello to February, a month of expressing
Love across the world, to those we love,
We will welcome you every day with
Sweet love as a reminder that
We love you.

When Love is Divided

When true lovers are divided,
The heart is still with pain that
Lingers in the heart, because
They lost their true love.

No one seems to care to hear my sad song.
All my friends have turned away without care.
I believe they were never my friends
at first because those who truly love you
Would care. Those who you thought
didn't care, stood by your side, when you
Give all your heart and soul you're
Empty as a shell.
Washed upon a shore.
Waiting for the tides at sea to wash away your tears.
Your drifting mind wonders where you are or
Are you lost at sea?
I pray when the tides roll in again, we will join
Together as one. I will welcome
You with open arms,
 and whisper in your ear

While the Moon is Bright

While the moon is bright,
I can see the heaven's light.
I can see the beauty in your eyes,
light heaven's light.
I know you want to go out of my life
But it's hard to let you go
Please give me another chance
To prove my love to you
I am blue, and lost without you in my arms.
Baby come back, I miss you.
My love is true.
In my heart, no one can ever take your place
Cause I love you.
Your sweet love has me bound in chains, because
I only love you.
I miss the fingers of your touch.
Your hands are softer than a baby's skin.
Let us start over again and give us two
Another chance.
No matter how gray your hair may be,
My love will never change.
I will always look at you as my childhood love
Tear stains in my eyes still cry
waiting for you to come back and wipe my eyes with your
    hands.

Mother's Day

Mother's Day is truly to remember
Even if you forget a gift
Keep good thoughts
for she is the only mother you'll get.
Remember all the things she's done for you.
Keep her warm inside your heart.
Your life will be filled with joy.
She is filled with love, joy, every day
Never forget a Mother's Day
She is the first who held you in her arms, like a blanket
Silky and warm.
Her love will never grow cold
Because her heart is warm.
She will always be good to you,
when no one else is there.
You don't get one, or two, who
Is really true
Mother's Day is a day
Of special love, and good thought just
For her alone.
You are the best in all the world, a gift
From God to me.
I love you mother, with all my heart.

Father's Day

Father's Day is a joyous day,
Locked up in my heart.
All the things that are in my heart
Is my love for you.
Memories of love, years that passed has been a
Special bond between Father and son.
I remember the day you taught me
how to love, and honor you
As a father that blessed me with
A strong man with power to raise his family as
A good man should.

I remember all your struggle
raising your girls and boys,
teaching us to love one another, even though we
Fought as boys do,
Your belt will always be remembered as a
Token of love,
To make us respect you.
Though your life was hard, you always put your children
    first,
and that's why I love and respect you with a special love.

The Stars

The stars did twinkle out in the heavens,
Like a holy night.
A guide for the wise men to
Find their way to the place christ laid in a
Barn far away. The star twinkles with lights
Glowing in the sky,
On Christmas night his star lights up
The earth with a heavenly glow.
The star shined down where he laid, like a
Crystal glow, his face was like an angel from above,
As he laid in the bed of hay.
The shepherd bowed to give him praise,
Glory, to the newborn king.
Mary was filled with joy,
For the newborn king,
the sheep, cattle looked upon him
With wonder upon his heavenly glow
Shepherd presented gifts of fragrance, gold.
The smell of pine trees filled the air
Joy filled the air, tonight we celebrate the day
Christ was born.
A gift from God.

Birds Outside the Window

Birds outside my window
Come catch spring with joy.
They sit in my tree
singing songs for me,
They sing a sweet melody in my ears
A special song
Pleasant for me to hear
From my window.
They come from the south each year
To visit me every year
They will always be my song birds
With many wings of beauty.
They nest in my tree
Beneath my window,
With new birds in the nest.
They are blue like the heaven's sky
They stay all summer vacation
With me each year.
I enjoy hearing their heavenly songs of God.
I will miss them when winter comes,
but they will always come back each year.

A Little Christmas Tree

Little Christmas tree sitting on a lot
Wonder if it was waiting on me.
It's short and bushy
The little tree looked so cold sitting in the snow.
I want to take it home with me,
I will dress it in silver bells, bows,
Rap it garland as a dress
For Christmas day.
With bright lights of the
Rainbow, and sit it in the window
for all children to see,
A star will sit upon the top like
The star in heaven.
Little Christmas tree
I love you with a special love,
Because you love me.
Santa will bring toys to
Sit beneath you, just for me,
Christmas tree you were lonely like me,
Cold on a lot, but now
I'll plant you in my yard,
so you will never be alone,
now you have a home with me
every day of the year.

Peace of God

Peace, may God be with you
In everything you say and do,
There will always be peace in life
For you, when you
Love one as yourself.
When you smile with joy,
You bring happiness to
A frown that's blue.
Bring peace with a smile to all who greet you.
A good day, spread heaven's love to fill the earth
With joy. It only takes a moment to smile.
When others are sad and blue, lift up the joy of the
    heavens,
Light up the world with laughter,
Let it ring out with joy, let the peace of
God fill the earth with
His praise,
He has made the earth with his hand
To make us a home on earth
All of his beauty is made
By his own hand.
The streams of the rivers flow in peace
To create ocean, sea,
For creatures to swim below.
The beauty of his flower that
Dresses the earth,
Their nests in the evergreens with
Babe of every birth,

The grass spread like a green carpet
To set down in the sun. Shade trees
blossoms of every color
To make the earth smell sweet.
He has given us peace and beauty
To bring comfort to all mankind on earth.

My Childhood Days

I forgot to say goodbye
To all my Green Street friends.
Every day has brought joy
To my memories
Like a treasure chest of gold.
God has blessed us with precious pearls
Of everlasting friendship,
Only found in heaven.
A Godly love to treasure inside
Our hearts that have been
Given by his hands.
Love roots like a tree
And blooms over the years as we grow.
In our hearts has developed
An everlasting friendship that will never end.
Our minds will always travel back to our
Hometown on a little street
Liberty Ave
15001

Peace Be with You

Peace be with you in
Everything you do.
Peace is like love that spreads happiness all
Around the globe.
Touching every heart that's blue.
Peace spreads laughter and joy,
Harmony with a smile.
Family gathering on holidays filled
With seasons of the past, when
We were young, old,
The smell of wood crackling,
Fire, the glittering spark
Flying in the air,
Like stars and lightning bugs.
Peace be with you in every season,
May we feast
Toast with joy.
Let the olden days always be a reminder
Of when we roasted on open firewood
Burning of the hearth.

God Be With You

With peace may God be with you
In hard times, and good,
Let his blessings flow in your life
Like a river. Let it flow like the spring rains.
Let it flow in due season, and out
Let the strong breeze blow in
With the peace of God,
Everywhere you go.
Let peace rest on your shoulders
As you trail through this world
Knowing God will always be by your side.

Mother

Mother's Day is always to be remembered.
Never forget to give a gift from the heart.
You're the child of her womb.
Loved and cherished in her arms,
She is the sweet smell of flowers
That filled the room of your birth.
While angels stood at your bedside,
To give her the gift of love.
Showered with thanksgiving and love
Her birth pain brought you in this world
To care tenderly with love.

Stars in the Heavens

Stars twinkle in the heaven's night,
To guide wise men to Christ,
The new born child.
The star was the pathway in the sky led to
The manger, above his head in the sky
The star sat still above
The manger and led the shepherd
Thousands of miles to Christ.

Gifts of gold, silver were placed before the crib.
Jesus laid under the heaven's light
Brighter than the stars.
God has given the world a king
To rule the world.

My Love

My bride, I love giving you
Everything a woman can desire,
The ring for a queen and diamonds for your precious love.
The church bells rang in the tower
The glad sounds of joy
Heaven joined us together
With a song of eternal love.

Flower of blue roses at your feet
Where a queen can walk with pride.
Yet you have given me the love I will cherish
Like a king forever

Gifts Under the Tree

Gifts under the tree
Wrapped in multilabel colors
Which should I open first or last
Mother and dad have been so kind,
and Santa's my best friend.

Voices singing in my ears,
It's the season To be jolly.
Family and friends
Feasting on Christmas day.
We were very poor
But rich in spirit
One or two gifts for tweets
Little elves like ours
That tree lights up my heart
With thanksgiving bells,
Blue and glittery
In the dark

Jupiter

Jupiter, so far out in space
I look upon you with my face
Wondering if there's true love in outer space.
I see you shining like a giant star
A glowing out in space, so far.

If there is true love out there
I'll take a rocket ship to love.
I wish upon Jupiter in hope for better love

Somewhere out there, I believe, is true love
To fill this lonely heart of pain
with the joy of love.

The Shadow of Love

The shadow of love comes within the heart
Seeking to find a friend to love
Waiting in the shadows of the night
Hoping to find love that's right

Let not another day pass by without love
Fill my heart with the gift of love
Arms that embrace me
With heaven's love

Hold me in your arms until daylight comes
And fill my heart with love.

John F. Kennedy

Kennedy was a great president
In my memory he lives in my mind
With great pride and love.
His death I recalled in high school
Every classroom filled with tears
And grief.
His love for the nation
Is still embedded in our hearts.
He is dead, but the memories of one of
The greatest president's voice sounding in my ears
Was one man whose heart was of gold,
Who lead us through life with pride
And leadership in the white house where
God gave men power to rule
This nation through the storms and battles of life
I thank God, for such a great leader that had
His people's backs through the battles of his life.

Happy Easter

Happy Easter everyone
I hope you receive a basket of candy
And toys and eggs painted like
The rainbow in the sky
There's an egg in the nest hiding for you to find
Jelly beans and chocolate bunnies taste so sweet
All your friends and family can have fun playing
In the grass, finding hidden candies and treats.

I hope your Easter is filled with many good things to eat.

Thankful for Easter

I'm thankful for Easter
There's a smile on every girl and boy
Easter parades to show off your Sunday best,
Girls' lace dresses in every color, fashion and style
Pretty bonnets and ribbons on their heads
Patent leather shoes and ruffled socks,
Boys dressed in suits, bow ties, and shiny shoes,
Brand new children dress up to celebrate the rise of the
    King,
Which is the reason for Easter day celebration.
New clothes and candy baskets to share with friends,
Family and finding the true meaning of Easter is a blessed
    day.

Little Stream

Little stream that runs by the meadow
Where are you going?
Filling the thirst of dry lands, valleys
To bring life to seeds and flowers
Filling water holes that mankind can
Drink from, and animals in the fields to fill their thirst

I see the roots of small and tall trees reaching the heavens
    one day.
I run to the ocean, sea and creeks that have flooded over
    the land
I refill all day as my duty here on earth
The grass needs me for its green fields to bring out its
    beauty in summer.
I am a life flowing stream of God's heaven
Giving water for the thirst of mankind.
I am like the streams
Of mercy that give life
To all God's creatures.

The Stair Steps of Heaven

On the stair steps
That lead to heaven, angels' golden wings are spread
Like big white clouds leading to the throne of the eternal
   God.
Flowing from earth to heaven with its graceful beauty
Glittery like fine gold trimmed in silver.
Heaven welcomes you by grace and love with
Open arms.
The stair steps of salvation lead to his eternal throne.
Where angels lift their golden wings in praise to welcome
   the saints of God.

Joe Louis

Joe Louis the champion of the world
If he hit you with a right he would knock you out.
If he would hit you with a left he would send you on a
    flight out of sight.
They call him the brown bomber who could blow down a
    man with his power.
He was the man with iron hands.
His name was spread with fame throughout the land,
He was faster than lightning,
No one could beat the champion in his days of glory.
He was like Robinhood, stealing everyone's hearts
He knocked out every opponent that came out of the
    corner ready for fame,
The champion was ready to knock down with one blow.
He was swift as the wind, no one could escape his blow.
The heavyweight champion in his day
That would take on some of the greatest men
That stepped into the arena for a fight.
His fame is still read in the halls of fame.
His picture captured in glory and fame.

Love is Like a Rainbow

Love is like a rainbow,
promising a bright future of eternal love,
 promising love that comes from the heart,
where two hearts beat as one, joined by God.
For every promise, their hope of eternal love,
If only lovers stay true to each other.
The flames of fire will not blow out when you add joy to
    the heart,
When you make it heaven on earth, promise it will always
    last forever.
After many years of building a house for two,
A nest of love will be strong enough to stand the test of
    time
That will create our rainbow in the sky.

Little Brown Cow 2

Little brown cow in the meadow, why are you alone?
Where are your friends, kin?
Why did they leave you alone?
The wolves have taken the home and left me all alone.
The nights are full of fear, no one to keep me warm.
Shadows of the night make me so afraid, the voices of the
    night are loud and clear.
I shake and shiver with fear,
There's nowhere to hide in the open space through the
    night
I need the warm milk to warm me.
And all of my lost friends to cheer me on.
I see bright lights in the sky, only the heavens comfort little
    me
The little brown cow.

I Am the Man in Your Dreams

I am the man in your dreams.
Step into my world of fancy,
you'll find love that's faithful and true.
A world where love is created by heaven,
in the chambers of love
You were meant for me, before life began.
You're just waiting to come into my life,
you're my queen on my throne, I bow down to you.
The king of hearts that will provide and protect you with
    my life.
There are no rubies or gold that compare to your love,
you are the treasure chest of my heart.

Rose

A rose blooms in spring,
The smell of sweet perfume fills the air.
Lovers are enchanted by its glorious power to make them
fall in love.
The birds and bees enjoy the nectar,
The pollen of love is spread throughout the forest,
where new flowers bloom forth with beauty.
Flower blooming like every color of the rainbow,
A parade of flowers of every size in beauty
For everyone to smell its beauty and glory,
Butterflies like to flap their wings and dance and taste the
sweetness of honey.
Mankind gaze on the beauty, with a smile to welcome
them in spring.
Roses are heaven's gift to dress the earth with beauty and
rebirth.

The Gift of Wisdom

God has given me the wisdom to know he is God and
   there is no other God.
He has given me strength to walk in his footsteps,
and to know right from wrong in his eyes.
His love is eternal, and everlasting,
He created me in his image because he wanted me to
   become the son of God.
He wants me to live in peace and harmony with others,
   and love them as myself.

The Little Tree

Little tree bending in the wind.
How can I help you grow stronger,
with the branches of my hand?
I will hold you up until it rains.
You are weak, but God is strong.
He will send his rain to fill your thirst.
One day you will be strong like me,
and your roots will drink from the spring streams,
and water holes in the earth.
Keep the faith, little tree.
One day you will be strong and stand high towards
    heaven's sky.

Stars

Stars come out at night and make heaven right
and make the earth shine bright
Stars come out at night and kiss the moon good night.
The stars glitter and shine bright.
While lovers make love under the moonlight.
Stars come out at night, and hide behind clouds all day.
Some falling stars make a pathway to earth,
Burn in flames to light the darkness at night.

My Home Town

Aliquippa, my childhood town
where all of my friends played
on the playgrounds with my best friends.
Baseball was our favorite game.
All our friends were our best friends.
Our old saying, it took a village to raise a kid.
Every door welcomed you as family.
People loved one another, and helped all people.
As a close friend, Aliquippa is always a wonderful memory
    in my mind
that fills my heart with joy.
Growing up in my old house,
My friend visited every day until the street lights came on
    at night.
We told ghost stories and were afraid to go to bed at
    night.
We will have good memories until the day we grow old on
    the playgrounds.

Angels Sang

Angels sang at Jesus's birth in days of old.
He came to take away our sins.
Angels guarded the baby at night,
While shepherds laid before him gifts of gold and silver, fit
   for a king,
Heaven's stars shone bright in heaven.
Light up the sky with a heavenly light.
God is a glory filled earth
with the blessing of the holy child's power
and glory was given to this little child,
to rule the whole world one day.
We praised God for his great gift, given to mankind.
Angels sang at his birth, a heavenly song.
He will be our king to rule, and bring peace and joy to the
   world.

Fourth of July Fun

People celebrate the fourth of July with American flags
    flying in the sky.
Firecrackers sounding like booms lighting up the sky.
Music can be heard with marching bands in the streets.
People dancing and rejoicing with family and friends.
Picnic in the backyard with children playing games and
    having fun.

Mothers Day

Mother's Day is truly to remember even if you forget to
   give a gift.
Express good thoughts of love and appreciation
for all the things she's done for you.
For she is the only mother that you have.
You will never get another as good as her.
You don't get one or two,
but one who loves you true.

Joy

Joy comes every day.
The joy of God comes every day,
even when you're down and can't find a friend that comes
    your way.
We can't see it but it chases dark clouds away.
When bad thoughts make you sad, joy can make you smile.
When things are up and down, joy can get your feet on
    the ground.
Don't let sadness get in your way,
joy will bring you out,
 and make you shout with joy.

The Touch of Your Hand

One touch of your hand makes me strong each day.
Lift up the day, all day long, love come my way.
The touch of your hand makes me a loving man,
so don't take your love away.
One touch of your love makes me a happy man.
One touch of your hand makes me not do wrong.
When I am near you my hands are warm with joy and
    love.
Don't ever take away your hand because I love you so.

To Grow Old

To grow old is wisdom and full of loneliness, grace and
   love.
You may not have many friends at your side but you have
   much love to share.
So people spread your love, because we all need love,
   young or old.
When I am old I will carry my pride,
and think of all the love I can divide to everyone when I
   get older.
Life began as a newborn child.
You can treat me like a child with love and tender care.
Treat me like you wish to be treated because the old
   becomes young like a child,
who need love and tender care.

My True Love

My true love gives me peace, and joy,
You know I am a happy boy.
You set the world aglow.
That's why I love you so.
You make the moon and stars glow.
And the earth is filled with light all around that glows.

You

Girl you are so fine,
I had to make you mine,
you are so loving and kind,
won't you please be mine?
You are so fine like wine.
You are as sweet as wine,
with your beautiful lips
you're sweet as candy apples,
glazed with red on your lips.
Your eyes are blue like heaven's clouds,
your hair is blazing like the sun,
you know it girl, you are a dream come true girl.
You are my wish come true.

The Little Harp

Music from my little harp reached my friend's heart with
  love.
Every note says I love you from my heart to yours.
Music brings great joy.
WIth love and happiness, harps of the angels sing of joy
  from heaven
when Christ was born on Christmas day.

I Lost a Love

I lost a love.
I was sad and blue like a cloud.
My heart was in pain.
It was a shame who was to blame.
I am in pain.
Our love was not the same,
It was lost in a game.
You can call me my name but I am not to blame.
Heart broken in pain, life is not the same.
Our love has been thrown away.
So much misunderstanding stood in the way.
Don't send my love away,
I thought it was here to stay.
Sweet love I hope we find love again one day.
I know true love will always find a way.

Roses in the Garden

Roses in the garden, as pretty as can be, as you can see.
Only God could have made them, for you and me.
Roses in the garden are a sight to see.
They bloom in many colors as you can see.
The splendor of their beauty is for our eyes to see.

Listen to God's Voice

I love the evening of the day.
When all the earth is silently at rest.
God put mankind and beast in a deep sleep.
He whispers in their ears the directions to take in life,
The highway to heaven is open every day to eternal life.
He welcomes us to a better life.
Sometimes we close our ears to his voice,
and get lost along life's highway.

God, Maker of Pure Life

Why does the morning glow through the night
And stars dance around the moon at night?
Yet it never loses its light until day.
Why does it fade away in the sky
when the sun comes out behind the clouds?
Let me wear it to go hide.
It's always on time to give light to the sky.
We thank you God we are not always in the dark
because we know you are the maker of all pure light for us
    to see.

Falling Tears

Tears that fall make me so blue.
Tears broke my heart, that's why I am so blue.
Woman, I gave you all my love.
And all you gave me is pain.
Who was to blame?
Your love has lost its power to be true,
You left my heart broken and in pain.
You took away my life.
The memory of our love is still full of pain.

Let's Call Love

Let's call back the love we once had,
when we first met,
when we were young and in love.
You are my childhood love
Who has lost the true meaning of love.
Anger has filled your heart with greed and bitterness
and you forgot to love.
Please my darling, I hope you find your way back to me.
Let us call love to bring us back together again.

My Heart Hurts So Bad

Why did you leave me?
It hurts so bad.
Pain overtook me by surprise without a notice or a sign.
You have left me with a wondering mind,
Instead of telling me what was on your mind.
I know I am not a perfect kind of guy, but I always loved
    you.
You have put my heart in the lost and found
wondering when you will return and come back for me.
I will be waiting for your return, there's no other that can
    take your place.
You will always be my one and only love.

Queen to Wed

Diamond rings are shiny as stars that glow in the night.
Precious like gold, and pearls.
They shine like the twinkling of stars at night.
My love, give me your loving hands to be wed.
You are my dream come true.
I am your loving man.
I am your king at the throne who wants you as my queen
    to wed.
Will you sit beside me on the throne and be my loving
    queen to wed.
I will praise you throughout the land
You are my chosen queen to wed

America

America, so strong and true,
God gave his love to you.
Be strong and wise like the eagles.
Stay strong and wise.
Let your flag ride the winds of the heaven with great pride
beneath the sun and stars.
Let prayer be your guide to lead you to victory and love.
Uplift the flag to the sky like wings to fly high with truth
and pride.

Sun

Oh the sun shines brighter than the sun lamp.
The sun shines bright, giving light to the earth.
The sun is like candle light shining bright,
that can't be blown out in the daylight.
Only God has the power to let the sun shine all day,
for mankind to see the beauty of the sun shines like a
    crystal
to light up the sky and keep us warm.

The Cat

The cat just caught a rat,
He caught it by his tail, and gave him a little slap.
The rat bit the cat and gave him a big scratch.
The rat ate the cat's food and ran back in his hole, and
    took a little.
The cat was angry at the rat,
He fixed a trap and snapped his own paw in the trap.

Trust in God

Trust in God, and you'll find a beautiful life every day.
Get down on your knees and pray.
He will always lead your life in the righteous way.
Trust in God you'll find the righteousness of life,
with faith in him in your life.
With faith in him on your life's journey
He'll hold you under his wing.
I must warn you storms will come,
but he will be there to guide you the right way.
He will protect you all the way.

Jackie

Rain beat down on my window pane.
Jackie had to go outside another day to play.
But all the other children played in every rain puddle,
splishing and splashing having fun.
They all laughed and made fun
'cause Jackie couldn't come out to play.
She was sad and blue, with tears in her eyes,
It made the children sad and blue.
Jackie said don't cry, it will make me very sad.
She opened the window and said,
"I'm so glad you're having fun,
I can't come out because I'm sick and blue."

The Candle

The little candle that glows so bright,
sitting in the window to guide me through the night.
When you have lost your light, you can use my eyesight.

God Made You For Me

All my love for you is real.
You'll feel my magic touch on your lips.
I will make every fantasy come true.
You are for me,
my heart is waiting to open up for your love.
You are in my dreams,
in every star I see your face that lights up my heart.
You are my joy every day.
There is not a sad note in music that plays.
Play a song of love to brighten up my day.
You're the future of my destiny,
you are beautiful in the sight of heaven.
God made you just for me,
you are a diamond that twinkles in my eyes.
God made you just for me.

Sharing

Sharing is giving of yourself to help someone else.
Sharing is opening your heart to give love,
or material things,
without having a selfish need
that's not giving of oneself.
Sharing can be an exchange of a smile to a lonely heart
that brings joy in times of sorrow.
Sharing brings a smile when the world smiles back at you.

The Little Old Train

As I stood at the gates,
I saw the smoke from the train.
I had to wipe the smoke from my eyes.
The smoke from the little old train smoked up the whole
    town as it passed
it made a toot toot out of town.
As the smoke blinded my eyes and choked my throat,
the little old train puffed right on out of town.
The little train stopped outside of town
it whistled and said,
"all aboard"
a loud sound.

Fruitful Little Tree

The little tree bent in the wind,
every time I passed that way.
I pick fruit from your branches every time I pass your way.
I am glad you are there to get rid of my hunger.
And I pick fruit from your branches, old girl.
I hope you live forever, and they never cut you down.
Because you are so tasty and sweet.
I love to sit under you, and lay my head on earth's pillow.

Friendship

Friendship should last forever,
carry it to the next generation with love.
Friendship is like a love song.
Beautiful with true meanings.
Friendship is to love someone as you love yourself.
Friendship never dies, but it lives in the heart forever.
It's like a clock that never stops,
it keeps time with hearts.

A Tear Falls

When your tears fell, it broke my heart.
I didn't mean to do you wrong,
I meant to love you all night long.
When your tears fall it breaks my heart,
baby it's tearing me apart.
When tears fall it makes me sad,
baby, you know I love you.
Tell me we're not through,
'cause I love you.

Let's Fall in Love

Let's give love a chance to grow,
Let us take it slow.
Love needs love to grow.
Love is like a beautiful flower,
It needs roots to grow.
Seasons will bring strength to seeds
that grow in our hearts.
Let our love grow in winter and spring
We will know it's real.
Flower seeds will have bloomed with the roots strong
to last many years to come.
We find strength with love if we dont rush falling in love.
Let us test the season to see if it's true love.

A Rose to My Mother

A rose to my mother
my expression of love.
A rose of love.
A rose is the most beautiful flower in the world.
She deserves the very best flowers in the garden of love.
My mother stands out like a queen, robed in red, crowned
    in gold, riches and rubies.
Mother is my valentine every day.
She deserves a field of roses
for they are the most beautiful flowers made by God's
    hands.

Always Young

In my eyes you will always be young.
Let's get on the dance floor.
The music is out of sight.
Bring the sounds of the music my way.
Let's make an evening of love,
my pretty little thing,
Let us imagine we're young again.
We may never get this chance again,
we're on the time clock that never stops
being in love,
you are the only one I'll ever love,
in my eyes you will always be young.

Christmas

Looking through the eyes of a young child at Christmas,
I see my face,
I see myself as a little boy full of excitement and joy.
My eyes are as big as saucers,
Looking at all the beautiful toys in the store window.
Santa on his sleigh, reindeer galloping like horses,
    connected to his sleigh.
The snow is white like cotton candy.

Beautiful Christmas Tree

A tree that was tall as the store,
colorful as a rainbow with glittering lights that glow.
I was amazed with excitement,
I never saw so many toys
sing and dancing
the lights were a beautiful sight to see,
every color you could count was on the Christmas tree.
The beautiful bulbs glittering gold and silver was a sight to
    see.

Christmas Heaven

Angels with uplifted wings praising God,
dressed in silver, white and gold.
Toys of every young boy's and girl's dreams were there
    before my eyes.
My head was full of excitement and I almost lost my mind.
My head was spinning like a wheel, around and around.
I thought I was in Christmas heaven.

Joy Bells

Before the window, joy bells were ringing.
The chorus was singing Christmas songs.
I felt the joy of the Christmas spirit.
I thanked God, for his special day
and the joy God had even given,
the greatest among thousands of toys.
Baby jesus brought the spirit of Christmas,
a day we celebrate his birth.
I felt the joy of those who love Jesus.

Love Travels

Why does love travel from coast to coast?
Love travels with the seasons,
Love searches for true love that will last eternally.
Love is gentle, and heart breaking to make you blue.
Love brings joy to the heart that's true.
Love is an arrow that finds true love.
Sometimes it misses.
It aims to the heart - a bitter heart.
Love travels again to find true love.
That is the meaning of love.

Super Fine

My woman is super fine.
Her lips taste like wine.
She is every man's dream,
I thank God she is all mine.
She is so super fine
She is always on my mind.

No one can ever take your place.
You are my beauty queen,
I crown you with a king's love on my throne.
You are the queen of my heart,
you are the treasure chest of my life.
I thank God you are mine.
Super fine.

All My Love for You

I will give all my love to you,
if you promise to be true.
I am captured by your charm, and beautiful face,
Your eyes are ocean blue,
you know I love you.
Your lips are ruby red, like a rose, in spring.
All my love is for you,
no one can take your place,
You are my pride and joy.
Your body is shapely in all the right places.
I'm captured by your charm.

Your Love

Your love brings me joy like a summer day.
I am so happy and filled with joy.
Spring time will never end when you're in my arms.
The sun shines just for you
To bring you joy in the summer sun.
Heaven lifts its shade to bring you blue clouds of joy.
And not rain.
You are the stars in my eyes that shine,
when I look upon your beautiful face.
Heaven made you just for me to love.

All of the People Know

All of the people know that I love you.
I will never let you go, because you make my world glow.
You're the sweetest thing on earth,
you're the sugar in my tea.
All of the people know, I love you,
That's why my heart beats so.
Let's make a future, and fall in love,
because we were meant for each other.
God made you my special love.
Heavenly sent from above.

Love That Has Saddened Me

Oh love that has saddened me,
You have taken your love from me,
the love that I have given to you,
You closed the door to my heart.
You have left me lonely and blue.
I hope we can renew our love,
before our love drifts away at sea.
I'm saddened because you have changed
with the season of time.
I thought you would always be mine,
I have lost my true love,
but I believe there is still hope you'll return to me.

Why I Was Born

God made me in his image to serve his purpose for him.
I am a man made with his bare hands,
molded into his image,
sent from heaven above to do his will on earth.
Gifted with many talents to paint the blue skies of heaven
    and beautiful stars at night.
My poems sing of the praises of his creation in heaven and
    on earth.
The land, oceans, skies painted with blue clouds.
I was born to tell of his grace and beauty.

Let's Make Love by the Fireplace

Let's make love by the fireplace.
This is our night to make love in the moonlight
from the window shining in your lovely face.
Your eyes are like the stars shining in the night.
Kiss me baby and hold me tight.
I want our first time to be remembered.
You make me feel like a king on the throne,
when you hold me tight and kiss my lips.
I hope this moment lasts forever, my love.

Diamond Rings of Gold

Diamond rings sparkle like glass,
It's a beauty to behold on your lover's hand.
A Diamond ring is a symbol of love.
A Diamond sparkles like stars.
Diamond rings look like the corners of the rainbow.
Diamonds never lose their beauty.
Diamonds are a woman's dream come true.
Diamonds sparkle like the stars from heaven afar.
Diamonds are special beauty stones, meant for the one
    you love.

Love is Not the Blame

Love is not the blame,
True love is honest and true.
Love always keeps its promises, to love until eternity.
Love is ordained by God, maker of heaven and earth.
Love is meant to bond two people together until death do
     they part.
Love is a gift from God to those that are in love.
Love is joy and happiness to share with one another,
married or engaged to become as one mind and spirit in
     God.

Joy Comes Every Day

Joy comes to lift us up when we are sad and lonely.
Joy chases dark clouds away on a rainy day.
Joy always comes with a smile to make you laugh.
Joy makes music to a song of love to dance the night away.
Joy dries up tears hidden in the rain,
Joy draws back the shades to see the sunlight shining
    bright,
Joy is summer days, full of fun and laughter.
Joy brings people together when winter turns into spring,
And flowers bloom everywhere in beauty.

Watch Your Steps

Watch the way you walk through life with so much pride
Because pride comes with a fall, when your head is always
    in the air.
Pride never carries a smile, but a frown, all the time.
Pride is a busybody that knows everything is right in his
    eyes,
But he is blind as a bat.
He has ears, but doesn't listen to the wise man,
Because he's smart in his own blind eyes,
He stumbles on a log with his eyes wide open.

Growing Old

Age comes with wisdom and grace, In God.
Many friends have passed and you are all alone.
Sometimes people don't realize that you are still alive,
They pass your doorstep without kind words, as if you
were a stranger in their eyes.
The nights grow longer and the moon isn't bright in my
window,
The stars have lost their twinkling glow.
In my mind, I see the beauty of heaven and earth, because
the holy spirit is in me.
He is my eyes to see everything he has made with his
hands.
His love surrounds me and the peace of God rests on my
shoulders.
I can run through the playgrounds, like when I was with my
family and friends as a young child.
I am born again in the eyes of God, because I am never
alone,
God is my eternal friend.

Lost and Found

You'll never know how much you love someone until
    they're gone.
A place at the table is empty, their plate is not there.
You can hear the voice of the loved ones in your mind.
Your fears are like rain that never stops.
But one day the sun will bring out a new day, and the dark
    cloud will pass away.
The sadness of your lost ones becomes a reality of life,
One day we will see them in heaven and we'll dance and
    rejoice as children of God.

www.ingramcontent.com/pod-product-compliance
Lightning Source LLC
Chambersburg PA
CBHW060333130626
46553CB00003B/996